And Yet

Also by Kate Baer

What Kind of Woman

I Hope This Finds You Well

And Yet

Poems

Kate Baer

HARPER

An Imprint of HarperCollins*Publishers*

Some of the material in this book has been previously published in another format.

HarperCollins books may be purchased for educational, business, or sales promotional use. For information, please email the Special Markets Department at SPsales@harpercollins.com.

FIRST EDITION

Designed by Jen Overstreet

Library of Congress Cataloging-in-Publication Data has been applied for.

ISBN 978-0-06-311555-2 (pbk.)
ISBN 978-0-06-311557-6 (library edition)

22 23 24 25 26   LSC   10 9 8 7 6 5 4 3 2 1

for the ones who feel like home

To be running breathlessly, but not yet arrived, is itself delightful,
a suspended moment of living hope.

—Anne Carson, Eros the Bittersweet

Making bank, shaking hands, driving 80
Trying to get home just to feed the baby

—The Highwomen, "Redesigning Women"

My Ambition Goes Off to War

Bored of bad moods and winter
gloom, my ambition goes off to war.
Bags packed to the nines, glitter heels
stuffed between cotton sheets and
army green. I didn't think they needed
glitter heels in war—but no one blinks
at the train when they're revealed in a
search, when the commander finds them
looking for any sign of trouble.

The train leaves, smoke dulls into the
clouds. I beg for postcards that never
come.

How to Be Happy

1) Wake up to the sound of the ocean
   on your white noise machine. It is too expensive

2) To do the real thing, you must swing your legs
   out of bed and shout "Ah! I am alive!" with just enough

3) Jubilation at the small things: coffee, cream, banana,
   the way your son pronounces cauliflower like

4) Call a flower by what it is: a little rage. Remember
   her bloom is not performing. Remember before you

5) Begin your big, important life

True Grit

Out and about, we ask our friend
how it was at the shore at her family reunion
and she says, *well*—and tries not to say
my horrible parents & *my horrible sister*
even though we all know the sound of
the car door slamming.

It is possible to leave out almost everything
in any given story. Like at my parents'
when I hold my hand like a gun and
pull the trigger or when we gather
in the backyard playing and call it
a really good time.

If You Were to Ask for the Secret to a Happy Marriage

after Leah Naomi Green

I would tell you how the fire beetle mates
only when the chaparral is burning.
How the prologue changes when you
write the second act. How even when
a room is backlit by the joy of children,
by the brilliance of a fantasy,
there will always be a death
dressed as a question, waiting alone
in that godforsaken dark.

Beach Body

Mountain body. I don't want your
[cropped body]. Give me all the hot
body. Soft body. Curve and dimple
big body. Love to see a strong body,
loose body, other kind of built body.

Want to hear your loud body. Lover-
in-the-night body. This is not your
mother's body. And even if it was—
look at how she moves.

Late Summer ~~in a Global Pandemic~~

The weeks are long, and all my son
wants is a new skateboard and a different
mother. I will not let my daughter eat a
bowl of bad strawberries, so this really
seals the deal.

They write on a scrap of old note paper:
Can you jest be nice?

A train pulls in, parks below my throat.
If only we could put the world on hold.

There Are Days

There are days I can't believe we let the boys
with the new blue jeans and slick haircuts
decide the emotions of fourth grade girls.
And how those boys grow into Fall Athletes
and Spring Play Leads, all arms around our
waists and *can I call you baby* now that we are
thin. And how they follow us to college, haunt
our rooms with little deaths. How they slip
behind a desk to sign our paychecks, become
somebody's husband. Say: *Now that I have a
daughter.* How they climb and climb and
climb and climb.

Burnout

I can no longer participate in
world breastfeeding week
memes about tired mothers
nurseries dressed in millennial pink

I cannot discuss potty training
sleep schedules and noise machines
how to fix a 30-minute-meal and
keep our children healthy

I cannot take one more minute of conversation
on strollers or video games
your mother's cruel suggestions
what so-and-so says is her trick for
making time for daddy

no
I did not / will not / could not
know what it is to be a *good mother*
when *mother* is already heavy enough

MILF

Mother I'd like to face.

Mother I'd like to fail.

Mother I'd like to fight.

Mother I'd like to find.

Mother I'd like to fire.

Mother I'd like to fool.

Mother I'd like to free.

Poem About Someone Else

This poem is not about me.
She is not fat, loves God,
straight—all the way up to
the teeth. In the morning
she wakes up swan-like,
grass-fed, a bevy of doves
circling—just waiting for
her next achievement.

♀ Bad Woman

25 miles away

There is a woman in my town who is so pregnant with adoration, she floats across the room. She says—*sister, listen* and *you gotta be a goddamn bossbabe*. It is so inspiring, people weep at the chance to see her, take her cloak into their hands. They say, *you saved my life*. They are *eternally grateful*. Meanwhile I am pregnant with indecision. The Glenn Close of every circle. Is she good or is she wicked? The ever present question. But what if I told you the proof is in the pudding? Touch my hair. Mouth my skin. Give me hand over heart, hand over breast, while you pledge my name.

New House

We move in under clouds and wake up
to the rain. There are no waffles or cereal
bowls, so the children cry while I wade
through boxes to stall their disappointment.
Isn't this fun, I clap at the sight of their
books and pillow pets. The roof leaks,
my husband paints the bedroom a shade
of terra-cotta pink. I hate it so much
I close my eyes whenever I enter the room.

Invocation

If you don't shut your mouth, I'll shut it for you, says a mother
to her baby daughter. I have found myself in the wrong aisle at a
Target in an unfamiliar town. Soap is what I'm looking for, country
fresh, requests my husband (just go outside, I say). We have recently
moved to the country. It reeks of manure and hydrangea blooms.
I miss those days, I say to the tired mother (I don't, but Lord hear
this quiet prayer).

Influencers

To hear a child rage, big and
blaring, and see his mother
bend to give him quiet kindness.
To see the winter's sun move from
her tired shade. To witness one
life's miserable devastation and
see her reach, instead, for joy.

Postpartum Questionnaire

In the past 7 days:

1. I have looked forward with enjoyment to things
   - ☐ As much as ever
   - ☐ Though there have been times
   - ☐ I have lost my grip on this world and can no longer see what used to sit in front of me and

2. I have blamed myself unnecessarily when things went wrong
   - ☐ Occasionally
   - ☐ I try not to imagine there is someone better suited
   - ☐ To care for my infant who cries constantly is how

3. Things have gotten on top of me
   - ☐ No, I have been coping as well as ever
   - ☐ Most of the time I have been coping well
   - ☐ Yes, there are those times
   - ☐ I cannot cope at all

Young Mother

There is no schedule. Like the baby,
I am untethered and unknowing. I
wear him like a spare appendage.
In these years it is in vogue to choose
a kind of mothering—attachment or
otherwise. I choose a pacing tiger, a
milk-drained spud. I wear my heart
like a too-big sleeve, dragging it across
every surface. In the evenings when
the world bares its ugly teeth—we walk.
Down sidewalks and stairs, hallways
and the rims of crowded rooms.
When someone asks for my ambitions,
I have no answer. I only dream of sleep.

Ideal Heaven

When we get there, the angels sing
Cardi B in four parts to assure us
no one is taking any of this too
seriously. After all the paperwork,
I find my friends in a blue lagoon.
God I could really use a drink, I say,
forgetting where I am. We laugh so
hard we cry.

Invitation

They say do one thing a day that scares you—
but I say find someone else to scare.
Remove your face.
Break the bed with your morning loving.
In the evening, go down to the water
and wait for no one.
Let your life rest
on what is already good.

Still Married

The children are getting older and
I don't know how we ever managed

with the dark nights and heavy car-
seats and babies nursing at my bleeding

breast. Nothing is easier and yet
here we are making pancakes
with the radio on.

Reasons to Log Off

The girl who said she could never eat a second slice
of pizza my senior year of college is doing really well.
My cousin posts a photo of a loaded gun. Have I ever
heard of the Second Amendment? Have I ever heard
of this new recipe? Cauliflower, a hint of lemon, some
chopped-up ginger root. Hey, do you want to lose
weight in only thirty minutes? Hey, can I have just a
moment of your time? Click here to receive a special
invitation. Click here if you want to believe in God.
Tomorrow there's a Pride walk to support the right to
marry. One comment says: I will pray for your affliction.
Another says: I hope you trip, fall down, and die.
Swipe up to find my new lip filler. Scroll down to read
why these four girls were horribly afraid. Greg is
asking for your number. Greg wants to send a
big surprise.

The Life-Changing Magic of Tidying Up

boys will be boys
she was asking for it
it's because he likes you

(goodbye)
(goodbye)
(goodbye)

These Days

We come in from a downpour
to find it raining indoors.

I don't know how to avoid it—

My body ages,
my anger burns into a seam.

I am so annoyed by love

and still it comes.

On a Thursday Afternoon

My son's friend tells him being gay is
an *abomination*, except my son hears
"a bomb in nation" and asks to hear
the sound.

It is easy to become a praying woman.

Dear God, let the children listen.
Let them take the world and press it
to their ear. And for every kindness,
every mercy, every blue jay rescued
from the thorns—

let your world bend to eagerly
return the favor.

On Mars

We eat on paper plates,
throw our trash into the lake,
fuck around with love. We are
free! free! free! No time limit
on the karaoke machine. You
choose Cher & I choose Jewel.
We haven't flossed in 20 years,
but it doesn't matter. After all—
this is the last of us out here

singing in space

Daily Planet

Babies are full of microplastics / New research shows / #MeToo isn't
going anywhere / You aren't ready for these Black Friday / Dealer shot
in front of wife and kids / Return to school deemed not safe for / Un-
vaccinated protests rise as / Hospital beds at capacity in these seven /
Places you can't travel until / Facebook whistleblower reveals / Ten
things you are doing / Wrongful death filed against police / Office
workers demand benefits / Billionaires pledge to give up / Oil spill
in California threatens / What we know so far

Too Late

The women came into focus like
thunder snapping at the heavens.

How easy it would have been
to open up both eyes.

The Worst Part

I take my sons down to the river to look for gulls, but instead
they peer down into the water. You can't see fish from here, I say.
But they do, several different kinds, and they reach to stroke their
backs. Begin to speak their language. It's not safe, I warn,
but it's too late: feet to fins, skin to scales. Their bodies sinking
into the water. Please come back, I beg, desperate for a net or hook
to bring them back to shore. *Help!* I scream to the other parents.
But no one moves, their eyes glistening as they clap, letting hope
be the better thing to believe in.

Grounds for Divorce

My husband recounts our children's births
like a camp counselor describing cold lake water.

It's not that bad
We pushed through
Actually kind of beautiful once you get used to it

Written Affair

after Mark Strand

I think of the innocent lives
of people in novels—
the high stakes, steady threat of
zombies, white women and their
murders, someone always
"padding down the stairs."
How powerless to be a woman written by a man
or a man written by a violence
or a child written by a need for a nauseating grave.
To find yourself held by the endurance of a comma.
To wake up every morning and never know
if the sea's a sea.

Childcare

How do I write about what decides
whether I live or if I die?

While I stood here writing this,
a siren rang. There's no one to go

but me.

Lists

For years I found myself so
unprepared for the world
that every week I'd make a list
of things to urgently adjust.

whiten teeth
shape up the eyebrows
lose 10 or 20 lbs

Last week I found a list
stuffed in a forgotten handbag.

We're all so vain and very sad.

L'esprit de l'escalier

Almost is the dead's least favorite word—
I *almost* laughed
I *almost* cried
I *almost* came
—quite boring if you think about it.
Like telling someone that when you were a child
you wanted to be a *veterinarian*.
Everyone wanted to be a veterinarian, Carl.

If not for the bacon, steak, and scallops
arranged on this little dish,
I would never come.

Awake

When an officer is asked to administer the death penalty, they are given two
or three days off to recover from what they've done. I think of this at night,
alone with my list of rude awakenings; how a mother finds her baby dead
without a reason, how a kindergartner feels at the sight of a loaded gun.
I admit there have been occasions when I've found it difficult to be alive.
To remember this in the wake of such injustice fills me with a shame I've
always known.

And Yet

there comes a time when you stop hoping for
One American Hero
and realize there is only you—
picking trash from the neighbor's yard,
hauling jars to the recycle bin,
calling your great-aunt Susan even though
she is not just *your* aunt Susan and
this is not just your godforsaken earth.

It is depressing to know a war is coming.
Worse to know the war will always be in you.

Little cauldron, little tender loon.
Take comfort in your bold heart
where hope and fear are mingling.

Baby Good

My friend's mother-in-law says her infant granddaughter has used up all her "baby good" when she cries in public. *It's time to go home*, she says at the restaurant while the baby cries and my friend swallows down her red wine and focaccia bread. *She's used up all her baby good*. And now it seems I've used up all of mine, in line at the store while the children wail, or at home when my husband asks where to find his sneakers, or at my high school reunion when a man asks if it's nice to have some hobbies with all those children. *Haha*, I say, and then I scream and scream and scream.

Can the Universe Be Poetic
Without a God?

It is inconceivable

the billionaire weeping on his deathbed
winter turning into spring
the daughter turning into her mother

without the hand of a bright and cinematic God

Thirties

I wanted everything.
It was obvious and everybody saw it
and talked about it with one another.

Idea

I will enjoy this life. I will open it
like a peach in season, suck the juice
from every finger, run my tongue over
my chin. I will not worry about clichés
or uninvited guests peering in my windows.
I will love and be loved. Save and be saved
a thousand times. I will let the want into
my body, bless the heat under my skin.
My life, I will not waste it. I will enjoy this life.

At the Covid Testing Clinic

I imagine the circumstances of my death—
my husband bent and weeping, my children
orphaned into little tremors of grief.

Mask it or casket says the woman to my
left. *Mother of four*, I text my husband.
Too easy of a headline.

They call my name, still alive for at
least another hour. *Yes I'm here*, I say.

I'm still here.

Headstone Suggestions

~~Loved and beloved.~~

~~Gone but not forgotten.~~

Honestly just a really good time.

When Someone Asks If I
Ever Think of You

I take the train at night, only a thirty-second ride
from bed to brain to half-sleep, its dim light

welcoming you onto the platform waving. We
hardly talk these days, too scared to disrupt the gods

who have agreed to let us share our dreams.
You take my hand, whisper something about the

weather, walk us to the door to Paris or the back-
yard of a wedding where we'll run into each other

after all these years. *It's your turn*, you say even
though we have no choice but to follow what's

left of memory into the dark.

Mourning Routine

I get up for the free drugs in the morning.
A little scroll scroll, swipe swipe, tweet and
delete. It's nothing but the stupidest thing
I've ever done. Top with coffee and now we're
headed toward an inconclusive terror made
from all the bad words from all the bad bros
and the loss of an all-important breakfast.
God help me, the children are calling! God
help me, there's nothing clean to wear. Time
to pull on something, trade my brain for
half a sandwich. It's just another day in the
good-bad, bad-good earth machine.

Bliss

She is reading, her soft body dead
against the sofa. Nothing moves
except the moon of her eyes.
The children in bed.
Her husband in bed.
The dog asleep against the oven.
Outside the wind howls, wolflike,
keeping the morning at bay.

Hot & Bothered

I search for homes for all my poems.
Walking down the street I say to every
stranger—Do you want this poem? To
the babies and the dogs and the UPS
driver holding flat screen TVs and
headphones wrapped in plastic. To the
bride walking from the church steps
and to the sister standing just off center,
hand on her throat. Do you want this?
I ask, searching for an answer. Trying
not to beg.

2022

we wear our troubles like a rouge
petrifying plum and rotten red
and sick-en-ing-ly salmon
are you okay? we ask our friends
oh yes, oh yes, it's been a year
like Groundhog Day if days were years
and years were bees
and Bill Murray was the kind of man
who'd never play piano
I dip my finger into the lake
run my hand through sand and weeds
I guess we'll garden
I guess we'll perish
I guess we'll walk down to the quarry
until the whole world
is finally painted red

Pandemic Christmas

Most years I am sick of the music by Dec 23rd.
I haul out to the car to turn on anything but
"Jingle Bells," or "Dominick the Donkey."

But this year I am lingering. Holed up in my
bedroom. Crying at the verse where Mary
sits weary in the moonless night.

Perpetual Doom

Come get your stuff! Mom messages
the family. In the attic, our childhood stacked
politely. Weathered dolls, cracked discs, a bag
of linens I've only seen late at night, riding
on the green balloon. *It smells like weed*, my
husband says on those nights, walking into
our kitchen. I hold my breath, think of my 80s
bedspread, and wait for a funny moment
to let out all my air.

January

it's one of those mornings
that looks like the night
couldn't get the darkness
out of its system.

The children,
asleep in their beds,
groan at the sound of me.

The cat stretches and moans
in her primitive tongue.

And I, the master of nothing,
walk through every room,
trying to remember
what comes next.

Revival

Dr. William Carlos Williams wrote poetry on his
prescription pad *to enliven the singularly sterile field
of science and philosophy.* I write mine on the backs of
my children. On the inside of my husband's mouth.
On any of these tame and routine days.

The Second Coming of Chr*st

It happens again. A 15-year-old girl
smart enough to know that shame
won't save her. Man won't save her.
God (in his infinite wisdom)
won't save her. Unless!
It was an angel! she says in her virginal jeans,
white shirt, a pair of sneakers
she borrowed from her cousin.

Blessed art thou among women
she tattoos on her wrist while
her mother cries and her father
stands out in a field nearby
just looking for a sign.

For My Sister

It looks hopeless because the hope
was sucked out of the room.
Kind of a good news / bad news situation.
The good news is there's a door,
the bad news is that it's difficult to open.

Do you remember when we were kids,
running down the hill,
not knowing if our legs could carry us?
That is how you must continue.
Wildly, wildly,
unafraid of what will surely come.

Anatomy Question

My son asks, if I could choose,
would I choose to be a woman
or a man?

Oh let me think, I say, not wanting to
offend him. Knowing I would always
choose myself.

History Repeated

Once the women realize they need only feed themselves—
Once the women realize they need only love themselves—
Once the women realize they need only birth themselves—
Once the women realize they need only employ themselves—
Once the women realize they need only pleasure themselves—
Once the women realize they need only themselves—

naturally, a revolution.

Help Wanted: A Bonus Wife

For immediate employment: woman between the ages
of 27 and 42, no experience required. Must be punctual,
dependable, cook like Picasso, bake like Van Gogh.
Duties include perpetual motion, detailed observation,
the ability to suppress a violent scream. You don't have
to be beautiful. You don't have to be anything but here.

Love Story

The wife sends her husband a blurry photo
of her left breast to signal that she will ███
under the conditions of dusk and wine.
He writes back: thumbs up, eggplant emoji,
yellow winking face. It is 2 p.m. on a Tuesday,
delicate and undistracted. By seven—
nothing but chaos and warning signs.
The children brawl at the sight of their beds
while the wife gathers up their blankets
and the husband fills their plastic cups.
I am a ghost, the wife says
when the children sleep and the moon
rises despite the threat of disappointment.
The husband nods, setting down the laundry,
and takes the ghost into his hands.

Both Ways

I walk down to the river of myself
and see what I have always known.
That as long as there is life,
as long as I am able to stand on my own two feet,
I will want more than I've been given.
I will want and I will want and
I will die trying to swallow every part
of this world. The hardness of any
man and the curve of any
woman and the mouth of
anyone open for something
other than a conversation.
I see so vainly then
in the reflection of my youth
that I would have myself
if I could stand her.

You ask me my intentions
but darling, I have none.
I only have desire.

In Line at the Coffee Shop
in a College Town

I want to know who's sleeping with their
boyfriend. Who's texting her professor
from a bathroom stall, a photo of her lace
bra. Who's clutching to their trust fund or
married to work study. Who's promising
their mother or abandoning their father
or sucking on the finger of a high school
love who's always showed ambition.

It doesn't matter where you go,
it's always some of this.

Out

It's hard for big-boned girls
to look small at the party—
the trunk of my body
knocking into tables, the corner of the loveseat,
trying to escape the conversation.

The stuffed fox turns his neck
while I slip into the bathroom.
The mercy of seven minutes.

Grief follows me
wondering what else
I'll let myself believe.

Not a Diet Diet

first the pitch / *not like the rest!* / the words of a left wing
celebrity / genetically disposed to a smaller waist / it's research
based / don't change a thing / until you cut out your distractions /
here's ten free tips on how to stop / giving in to everything you
crave / recruit five friends / sign for a year / this is your chance /
to find a better / be a better / you

Startled

It just so happens that you're presented with the chance to read a list of all the people who've ever hated you. It's quite long from what you can see. To help you decide, you compile a list of pros and cons. On one hand, you would know once and for all. On the other hand, you might just throw yourself off a bridge. It takes some deliberation, but eventually you decide to read it. You turn to the first page trembling, afraid of every traitor. Instead you see your own name, written over one hundred thousand times. Oh! you gasp. Startled doesn't even begin to describe it.

Summing It Up

We were born in June
even if it was actually December.
God said, Stand up and try.
And even if we couldn't stand
our mothers carried us.
We lived if we lived.
We died if we died.
What is the point?
everyone asked
since the beginning.
Since the very beginning of time.

Putting Away the Baby Clothes

It's delicate,
the edge of horror.

I have crossed
a thousand rivers.

How foolish we are
to believe what we love won't end.

40

Where are the poems
about stress induced erectile dysfunction,
how it is no longer in vogue to have
so many children, or about the wife
who cuts herself in two
because sometimes it is easier to
write yourself out of the play
than to face another breakfast.
It is easy to say *I love you*.
It is easy to move against yourself
in the quiet of an empty room.
In television shows, it is always
the wife who is unhappy.
Where are the poems
about the grief of two ordinary people
who fell in love.

Sunday Drive

In spring you can live anywhere—
any little town you drive through,

magnolias and redbuds blooming,
children dancing on the lawn.

You see the Victorians, the picket
fences. The library and corner stores.

We could really make a life here, you
might say. We could really make a life.

Sophomore Year

Smell of dorm wood and microwaves.
Girls dressed up like wives in training.

When he laughed, I knew I was
in trouble. *You will have a great life,*
he said. *None of this will matter.*

How strange it is when two things
can be true at any given time.

God at the End of the World

Even then, the people argued
and the poets wrote and the politicians
continued with their bad behavior.
But what of God? the prophets cried
while the mothers wept and the fathers
built barriers around the children.
It was in this way they drew a line through it
and didn't have to think about it anymore.

Writing Poems High/On Twitter

Discourse on a kind of writing—
I would rather die.
Discourse on a kind of parenting?
Jesus fucking Christ.
Jesus fucking Christ?
Sounds a bit problematic.
Some will write me off once they
get to that part.
The zealots will say, everything
she's ever said about gays.
Everything she's ever said about
how to gently care for children.
That can't be true after
Jesus Fucking Christ.
That's the problem with God, isn't it?
The ticket out of anything.
The cheapest ride
you'll ever take.

Oldest Trick

I ask my son, did everyone remember
to bring along their butt?
I don't want anyone to forget, I say
straight-faced, eyes locked,
or we'll have to turn around.

The thing is, to laugh would be
to admit their failure. But to hold it in?
Pure impossibility.

Of Marriage & Friendship & Faith

What it has always been
is a power struggle.
Sally Rooney wrote three books
about it. No one wants to admit it,
each one they are in,
for there are many.
But once it consumes you,
it will bring you to your knees.
It will reach around,
put its hands on your throat.
It isn't only Sally Rooney
by the way. I just knew it would
get your attention.

As for the Mother

1. She is a good mother.

2. She will fill up any empty room.

3. She does not want.

4. She does not lie down in greener pastures.

5. She will be not be denied

    a. unless she denies

    b. unless she denies

    c. unless she denies

6. She restores the soul.

Without a Moral, There's Just a Happy Woman

A woman wins a Powerball jackpot of 100 million dollars. She has always dreamt of having money. The woman grew up poor. Her mother made cans of Spam for dinner and her father would wear his shoes until they split open at the bottom. Even then, he would try to tape them together. It never works, Bob, her mother would say when she still spoke with tenderness.

I want it all in cash, the woman says to the Powerball jackpot representative.

At home, the woman tells her husband she is going on a trip. What kind of trip? he asks, not looking up from his recliner. Her trunk is packed. Her cupholders stuffed with hundreds. Even the woman's bra bulges with wads of lucky green. I am going to be so happy now, she says to the rearview mirror.

Days pass. Winter moves across the valley. The truth is, you wouldn't believe how happy she is now. The happiest woman you'll ever meet.

As the Day We Were Born

There are times I long to be good. It sneaks up on me
like a lady in an elegant coat. She says, what could you
possibly be doing here? And oh, how shame fills me.
Cemeteries of regret returning to their proper form.
But what of the Arctic Tern, a voice says from some-
where deeper. The Sooty Shearwater. Migrations of
a dreamer. No hat or coat to speak of.

Glue

The length of my husband finds me
the evening of a winter storm.

The room is cold but the carpet warms
under the persistent stimulation.

If not for this, I do not know
how we could hold the things we carry.

The Garden of Eden:
Updated Jacket Copy for the Modern World

Adam, the original *man's man,* &
Eve, the original *desperate housewife,*
find themselves in quite the pickle
when a serpent salesman asks Eve
to take a bite of a juicy secret.
A harrowing tale of love, lust
& the presence of a clever Master
who pulls out all the stops
to reveal a dark and rueful world.

Most Likely Scenario

I take a train down to the bottom of the ocean.
The devil meets me there, hands me a pair of
slippers. Says, *if only I had the time*, when I talk
about my books. Out in the water, a dolphin turns
to watch my big departure. I thought this would
be different, I say into the mic. The fish laugh
and turn to wave their fins goodbye.

Just Like Us

I see a writer from the Most Prestigious Program
slink into the room, pull out her phone,
and search for a name in the Metaverse.

There is a temptation for the poets
to write as if they haven't lived in the
modern world. But give me more of this.

Birthday Girl

Your appetite changes.

You go down many spirals
hand built on your inheritance of lust and rage.

Much time is spent pondering the merits of a fortune.
What it means to be both citizen and animal,
animal and one who's watched from a tiny screen.

There is a light at the end of most your tunnels,
but we both know that can only last so long.

For My Children

What does the world require of you?
Nothing.
So find in yourself what you require
and go.

Sweet Spot

Love on the weekend.
The soft orchestra playing in
your hands with the low strum of cello
and desperate adherence to the social constructs
of a hardware store.
At home, the counter begs for some attention.
And to the violins we are
denied, deny.
Your animal body and
the woodwinds climbing.
Back against the bedroom wall,
a single word enough
to bring in the sound of trumpets
while the percussion finds the drum
and the chorus sings their Hallelujah song.

Episiotomy

Nail on thumb.

Thumb on thorn.

Thorn held on a burning bush.

Still—there are good things in this world.

Requited thirst.

The thick spread of butter.

My husband's hand upon his heart

over this celestial joy.

Peter Pan's Advice

My son's tight grip around my neck.
Hot breath from lips of silk and honey.

On the edge of every grave I work to
sidestep—I hope I remember this.

Year Twelve

The night rose between us like a current.

You bathed the boys. I slammed the pots
into their corners.

To make from tenderness this institution—

how bold we are to find enough
to somehow begin again.

Butterfly Effect

If I open the door for the man
who screamed at our cashier:
you stupid fucking idiot
I've been a patron here all my life—
will he be redeemed?
~~If I smile~~
If I pull down my mask and smile
will he see how the flap of a butterfly's wing
can change the course of anyone's direction?
Here's what I want to know:
at the end of it all,
do we sit in front of a big projector
where everything, every flap,
every inconvenience,
is more than enough explained?

The Truth Is

You want a poem for the children.
Something to teach the children.
I don't know what I've learned,
isn't that the problem? With all
of this, they say to *trust your gut*,
but my gut is an ugly liar, ready
to intrude on unsuspecting
colds, unsuspecting doctors,
unsuspecting animals walking
across the unsuspecting porch.

We expect so much of children,
hovering above them like giant,
invincible gods. What a racket
to discover as an adult, how
little we have to pass down.

At Preschool Drop-Off

At preschool drop-off
we watch as the fathers march in with their children,
each with a different dressing style.

The one with the truck, I point.
Tight shorts, long hair, a bit thick
around the middle.

Everyone mortals differently,
my friend replies in the big group thread.
We all know it's a typo, but also—very true.

The Greatest Human Emotion

For Ann

The moment in the song

when the piano performs its resolution.

Dopamine of a savior.

Some say it must be love

or hope,

that wild and cardinal thing in all its feathers.

The answer much purer:

first breath of air

after being trapped under the covers,

the sight of your son's body

around the corner in the department store.

The doctor calling, dust devils of ash

in every peripheral view—

Your results look good.

No reason to worry.

[Relief, relief, relief.]

Astronomy Lessons

The night stretches out
like a cat after waking.
Have you ever seen so many stars?
I ask my son who is
too little to have ever seen
anything but the universe
I have placed before him.

What to Write After Another School Shooting

I start with my daughter's teacher. I write *oh my god*
and don't get any further. I imagine her body over
my daughter while her son sleeps at home in his crib.
So I write *thank you* and delete it. I write *I've been*
thinking of you and delete it. I write *shit shit shit*
and try not to delete it. Right now she's reviewing
division with the children. *I am so sorry*, I write in
the subject line. Somewhere outside the classroom,
not far if you really think about it, a child is being
buried. *Delete, delete, delete.*

Sad Olympics

To deal with my depression—I buy
a new air fryer, a pink diffuser, a junior
spider plant.

I don't want to be so broken-hearted,
yet sorrow walks into every room,
bangs on the piano.

Give me liberty, but hold the death.
There is only so much you can outrun.

Filling the Page

At a dinner party
one of the husbands says
it must be easy writing poetry.

Can't anything be a poem? he laughs.

You're right, I say, slipping off his shoes
& pulling out his molars—
searching for any crevice to insert
a semicolon
before I drag him over what is known as

this white

& provocative

space.

Personal Detention

I can't fix men with poems.
I can't fix men with poems.
I can't fix men with poems.
I can't fix men with poems.
I can't fix men with poems.
I can't fix men with poems.
I can't fix men with poems.
I can't fi x
          m
            e
                n

Dad

at the party where the food was bland

the company worse

and the weather

let's just call it all unpleasant

my father stood talking among my uncles

but when I walked over and said, *how long—*

he dropped his fork

folded up his paper plate

said, *I can leave right now if you want to*

I can take you home right now

Freedom Tour

On the field trip, your skin electric
with the possibility of death or a separation,
clutching your brown bag with one hand,
best friend with the other.
Who's ready to see the city? the driver grins.
Statue of Liberty or the Liberty Bell—
I can't remember.
Either way, grown-ups showing children
everything they should be thankful for.

Sewer Rats' Delight

There is a library in Brooklyn
where you borrow pianos instead of books.
It is cumbersome but always quite rewarding—
the sound of Für Elise as we approach
the subway stairs.

What Are We Doing Here?

I fake my bladder to avoid answering
a question on Global Warming,
the Modern Farmhouse, on
Misbehaving Kids. Instead
every evening, I ask my daughter—
What was your rose?
What was your thorn?
& she lists things she won't remember
thirty years later,
lying on her daughter's bedspread,
looking for something to believe.

End of the World

Have you always wanted a dog?
Get a dog.
Care for it with gentleness.
~~Walk along the edges of the hayfield,~~
~~singing.~~

Have you always wanted to sing?
Sing.

Mixup

In a cosmic mixup,

the wife switches bodies with her husband.

Nothing like this has happened before, she cries

as she pulls on his pants, minds the crotch,

barrels down the long staircase to an office where they call her

Bud & *How About Those Steelers*.

It's upsetting, the whole charade,

except at lunch when she orders fries and no one says,

We're so bad,

or at the meeting when she gives the room all her best ideas

and they say, *Man, where have you been?*

We have to fix this, her husband begs

when the wife returns for dinner.

Come here, she says, slipping off her shoes

and drawing the curtains

before she makes love to another life.

Halfway There

Whatever happens,
you are free to go. Free
to peel off what's left of this story and choose
another. It is not
too late.
It is definitely *worth the trouble*.

Remember the story of the lion
lost without his courage.
Too scared, full of fury,
the great wizard
standing in the emerald tower,
knowing the lion was already brave.

Marvel

To find you sitting at my kitchen counter
swinging your long young legs,
asking about the hummingbird,
where does it go when it rains,
& what kind of food will we have for dinner.
I have never met a more beautiful child.
When you were born I said to the nurse—
I do not know her.
You looked like an alien from another planet
and now you're here,
as if an angel appeared to Mary
and said *can you raise this baby?*
Except I am Mary and the angel
& you're the daughter who became a lion
in an otherwise soft and
ordinary life.

Fatal Flaw

I throw a surprise party for my rage.

Corner booth, a handful of first responders.

Thanks for coming, I announce,

slamming down my quarters.

Sometimes I think I must be

an insult to this world.

Once, a little drunk, I wrote *inslut*

and oh how I am both.

Too full of hope one moment,

too full of disgust the next.

Just check the weather or my poems.

Good today and bad tomorrow.

Like a dog following her tail—

and yet

and yet

and yet.

Acknowledgments

Tremendous thanks to my agent, Joanna MacKenzie, and my editor, Mary Gaule, for their unwavering support. To Beth Hicks and Hayley Silverman for their help with the audiobook. To my first readers and editors, Kary Wayson, Maureen Nolt, and Bethany Nissley.

Thank you to Amy Ross for the cover illustration and Joanne O'Neill for the cover design. To the team at Harper including Kelly Doyle, Megan Looney, Amanda Hong, Jen Overstreet, Amy Baker, and Lisa Erickson. I am so grateful.

Additional gratitude to the editors of *The New Yorker* in which "Reasons to Log Off" and "Mixup" first appeared.

There are several quotes from other, better poets in this book. Grateful acknowledgment below:

"Written Affair" quotes Mark Strand's poem "Fiction," and "If You Were to Ask for the Secret to a Happy Marriage" quotes Leah Naomi Green's "Field Guide to the Chaparral."

This book is dedicated to my friends and family. I know it sounds a bit generic, and yet without these women and handful of men, this and I and all my books simply wouldn't be.

About the Author

Kate Baer is the *New York Times* bestselling author of *What Kind of Woman* and *I Hope This Finds You Well*. Her work has also been published in *The New Yorker*, *Literary Hub*, *Huffington Post*, and the *New York Times*.

ALSO BY
KATE BAER

New York Times **Bestseller**

"Straight-up brilliant.
A collection of 'erasure poems,' the book sees Baer sifting through the thousands of messages she receives online via direct messages, social-media replies, and emails to then turn them into pointed rebuttals, biting retorts, and clever reconsiderations. Like turning straw into gold, Baer tosses her inbox on the spinning wheel and weaves a collection of poems that will speak to anyone who has spent even a few moments on social media. Instant 'like.'"

—SHONDALAND

AN INSTANT #1 *NEW YORK TIMES* BESTSELLER

"If you want your breath to catch and your heart to stop, turn to Kate Baer."

—JOANNA GODDARD, *Cup of Jo*

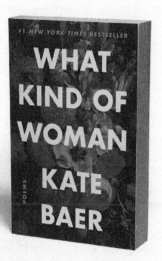